The Missions: California's Heritage

MISSION SAN JOSÉ

by

Mary Null Boulé

Book Fourteen in a series of twenty-one

DEAR READER,

You will find an outline of this chapter's
important topics at the back of the booklet.
It is there for you to use in writing a report
or giving an oral report on this mission.

If you first read the booklet completely,
then you can use the outline as a guide
to write your report in your own words,
instead of copying sentences from the
chapter.

Good luck, read carefully,
and use your own words.
MNB

The Missions: California's Heritage

MISSION SAN JOSÉ

by

Mary Null Boulé

Merryant Publishing
Vashon, Washington

Book Fourteen in a series of twenty-one

With special thanks to Msgr. Francis J. Weber, Archivist of the Los Angeles Catholic Diocese for his encouragement and expertise in developing this series.

This series is dedicated to my sister, Nancy Null Kenyon, whose editing skills and support were so freely given.

ISBN: 1-877599-13-1

Father Junípero Serra

INTRODUCTION

Building of a mission church involved everyone in the mission community. Priests were engineers and architects; Native Americans did the construction. Mission Indian in front is pouring adobe mix into a brick form. Bricks were then dried in the sun.

FATHER SERRA AND THE MISSIONS: AN INTRODUCTION

The year was 1769. On the east coast of what would soon become the United States, the thirteen original colonies were making ready to break away from England. On the west coast of our continent, however, there could be found only untamed land inhabited by Native Americans, or Indians. Although European explorers had sailed up and down the coast in their ships, no one but American Indians had explored the length of this land on foot . . . until now.

To this wild, beautiful country came a group of adventurous men from New Spain, as Mexico was then called. They were following the orders of their king, King Charles III of Spain.

One of the men was a Spanish missionary named Fray Junípero Serra. He had been given a tremendous job; especially since he was fifty-six years old, an old man in those days. King Charles III had ordered mission settlements to be built along the coast of Alta (Upper) California and it was Fr. Serra's task to carry out the king's wishes.

Father Serra had been born in the tiny village of Petra

on the island of Mallorca, Spain. He had done such an excellent job of teaching and working with the Indians in Mexican missions, the governor of New Spain had suggested to the king that Fr. Serra do the same with the Indians of Alta California. Hard-working Fray Serra was helped by Don Gaspár de Portolá, newly chosen governor of Alta California, and two other Franciscan priests who had grown up with Fr. Serra in Mallorca, Father Fermin Lasuén and Father Francisco Palóu.

There were several reasons why men had been told to build settlements along the coast of this unexplored country. First, missions would help keep the land as Spanish territory. Spain wanted to be sure the rest of the world knew it owned this rich land. Second, missions were to be built near harbors so towns would grow there. Ships from other countries could then stop to trade with the Spaniards, but these travelers could not try to claim the land for themselves. Third, missions were a good way to turn Indians into Christian, hard-working people.

It would be nice if we could write here that everything went well; that twenty-one missions immediately sprang up along the coast. Unfortunately, all did not go well. It would take fifty-four years to build all the California missions. During those fifty-four years many people died from Indian attacks, sickness, and starvation. Earthquakes and fires constantly ruined mission buildings, which then had to be built all over again. Fr. Serra calmly overcame each problem as it happened, as did those priests who followed him.

When a weary Fray Serra finally died in 1784, he had founded nine missions from San Diego to Monterey and had arranged the building of many more. Fr. Lasuén continued Fr. Serra's work, adding eight more missions to the California mission chain. The remaining four missions were founded in later years.

Originally, plans had been to place missions a hard day's walk from each other. Many of them were really quite far apart. Travelers truly struggled to go from one mission to another along the 650 miles of walking road known as El Camino Real, The Royal Highway. Today keen eyes will sometimes see tall, curved poles with bells hanging from them sitting by the side of streets and highways. These bell poles are marking a part of the old El Camino Real.

At first Spanish soldiers were put in charge of the towns which grew up near each mission. The priests were told to handle only the mission and its properties. It did not take long to realize the soldiers were not kind and gentle leaders. Many were uneducated and did not have the understanding they should have had in dealing with people. So the padres came to be in charge of not only the mission, but of the townspeople and even of the soldiers.

The first missions at San Diego and Monterey were built near the ocean where ships could bring them needed supplies. After early missions began to grow their own food and care for themselves, later mission compounds were built farther away from the coast. What one mission did well, such as leatherworking, candlemaking, or raising cattle, was shared with other missions. As a result, missions became somewhat specialized in certain products.

Although mission buildings looked different from mission to mission, most were built from one basic plan. Usually a compound was constructed as a large, four-sided building with an inner patio in the center. The outside of the quadrangle had only one or two doors, which were locked at night to protect the mission. A church usually sat at one corner of the quadrangle and was always the tallest and largest part of the mission compound.

Facing the inner patio were rooms for the two priests living there, workshops, a kitchen, storage rooms for grain and food, and the mission office. Rooms along the back of the quadrangle often served as home to the unmarried Indian women who worked in the kitchen. The rest of the Indians lived just outside the walls of the mission in their own village.

Beyond the mission wall and next to the church was a cemetery. Today you can still see many of the original headstones of those who died while living and working at the mission. Also outside the walls were larger workshops, a reservoir holding water used at the mission, and orchards containing fruit trees. Huge fields surrounded each mission where crops grew and livestock such as sheep, cattle, and horses grazed.

It took a great deal of time for some Indian tribes to understand the new way of life a mission offered, even though the

Native Americans always had food and shelter when they became mission Indians. Each morning all Indians were awakened at sunrise by a church bell calling them to church. Breakfast followed church . . . and then work. The women spun thread and made clothes, as well as cooked meals. Men and older boys worked in workshops or fields and constructed buildings. Meanwhile the Indian children went to school, where the padres taught them. After a noon meal there was a two hour rest before work began again. After dinner the Indians sang, played, or danced. This way of life was an enormous change from the less organized Indian life before the missionaries arrived. Many tribes accepted the change, some had more trouble getting used to a regular schedule, some tribes never became a part of mission life.

Water was all-important to the missions. It was needed to irrigate crops and to provide for the mission people and animals. Priests designed and engineered magnificent irrigation systems at most of the missions. All building of aqueducts and reservoirs of these systems was done by the mission Indians.

With all the organized hard work, the missions did very well. They grew and became strong. Excellent vineyards gave wine for the priests to use and to sell. Mission fields produced large grain crops of wheat and corn, and vast grazing land developed huge herds of cattle and sheep. Mission life was successful for over fifty years.

When Mexico broke away from Spain, it found it did not have enough money to support the California missions, as Spain had been doing. So in 1834, Mexico enforced the secularization law which their government had decreed several years earlier. This law stated missions were to be taken away from the missionaries and given to the Indians. The law said that if an Indian did not want the land or buildings, the property was to be sold to anyone who wished to buy it.

It is true the missions had become quite large and powerful. And as shocked as the padres were to learn of the secularization law, they also knew the missions had originally been planned as temporary, or short term projects. The priests had been sure their Indians would be well-trained enough to run the missions by themselves when the time came to move to other unsettled lands. In fact, however, even after fifty years the California Indians were still not ready to handle the huge missions.

Since the Indians did not wish to continue the missions, the buildings and land were sold, the Indians not even waiting for money or, in some cases, receiving money for the sale.

Sad times lay ahead. Many Indians went back to the old way of life. Some Indians stayed on as servants to the new owners and often these owners were not good to them. Mission buildings were used for everything from stores and saloons to animal barns. In one mission the church became a barracks for the army. A balcony was built for soldiers with their horses stabled in the altar area. Rats ate the stored grain and beautiful church robes. Furniture and objects left by the padres were stolen. People even stole the mission building roof tiles, which then caused the adobe brick walls to melt from rain. Earthquakes finished off many buildings.

Shortly after California became a part of the United States in the mid-1850s, our government returned all mission buildings to the Catholic Church. By this time most of them were in terrible condition. Since the priests needed only the church itself and a few rooms to live in, the other rooms of the mission were rented to anyone who needed them. Strange uses were found in some cases. In the San Fernando Mission, for example, there was once a pig farm in the patio area.

Tourists finally began to notice the mission ruins in the early 1900s. Groups of interested people got together to see if the missions could be restored. Some missions had been "modernized" by this time, unfortunately, but within the last thirty years historians have found enough pictures, drawings, and written descriptions to rebuild or restore most of the missions to their original appearances.

The restoration of all twenty-one missions is a splendid way to preserve our California heritage. It is the hope of many Californians that this dream of restoration can become a reality in the near future.

MISSION SAN JOSÉ

I. THE MISSION TODAY

Historians have often wondered why Mission San José was located as far east as it was. Maybe it was placed there to give missionaries better control of the warlike Indian tribes nearby. Or possibly it was to give protection to travelers crossing the mountains. Whatever the reason, it is the only California mission on the east side of San Francisco Bay. Nestled against the mountains fifteen miles northeast of the city of San José, it is now within the city limits of Fremont. Behind the mission buildings is a large convent. Ancient olive and fig trees line the back of the small piece of property still belonging to the mission.

For many years San José Mission was the only one in the California chain without either a replica or restoration of its old mission church. A small part of the original cloister was all that was left of the once huge quadrangle. In 1982, restoration of the mission church was finally begun. A miracle of recreation was to come to Mission San José!

After carefully removing a one hundred year old wooden church from the original foundations, work started on an exact replica of the 1809 adobe church. Great care was taken by local historians and the building contractor to make the restoration as close to the original as possible. Adobe bricks were not made by the old method, but were made of the same material and shape. These new bricks, however, were reinforced with asphalt so they would not "melt" in the rain as the original adobe had. 150,000 bricks were needed to rebuild the church. The walls were then plastered and painted a creamy white.

Old building methods were used as much as possible. Beneath the hand-tiled roof, modern builders used a two-hundred-year-old process of tying hazelwood branches together with rawhide thongs to form the under-roof. The branches can actually be seen under the church eaves. No square-headed nails are manufactured today, so the builder had each nail used in the building flattened by hand to give it the "old" look!

The church has a massive look to it, even though it measures but 126 feet long and 30 feet wide. Maybe it has this look because there are so few outside windows: three, to be exact. One tiny window is over the church entry doors and the two remaining windows are in the sanctuary, one on either side. Huge buttresses on each side of the four to five feet thick outside walls add to the immense look of the building.

The church facade has almost no decoration. Large dark-wood entrance doors are topped by a dark wooden gable. A gabled window above the doors is the only other decoration to the church front. The charm of San José Mission church is the lovely bricked half-circular steps leading to the church. Until digging for the restoration was begun, no one knew the stairs were there. Through the years dirt had completely covered the steps, and it was only when digging for foundations was started that the stairs revealed themselves. It was decided to cover the old worn steps with a layer of brick to keep them from crumbling, but the new layer did not destroy the graceful charm of the two sets of steps.

The bell tower is low, hardly showing above the church roof. The original designer of the church knew the dangers of a tall bell tower in earthquake country. Within the tower are four bells, all of them original. Three of the bells were used until the 1970s, when a wooden tower sheltering them became unsafe. The bells were carefully lowered and placed in the cloister museum until 1984, when they were hung in the newly rebuilt bell tower. The fourth bell is silver and was once described as having a "wondrous" tone. It was recast after it fell and broke in the 1868 earthquake. The bell was repaired and hung for many years in a church in Oakland. It was recently returned to Mission San José to take its place, once again, with the other three bells.

The inside of the newly rebuilt church is just as it should be. What a thrill to see how carefully the 1830s style is reproduced in the decorations. When the church collapsed in 1868, all work done by the famous Mexican artist, Augustin Davila, was thought to be destroyed forever. Davila had frescoed the walls in Mediterranean style, joyously painting marble columns and balconies along both side walls. Around the doorways he had painted the likenesses of marble pillars and gables. Richard Menn, the architect and restorer, has beautifully brought back Davila's style on the present walls.

Twelve Stations of the Cross hang on the windowless walls. The framed paintings are from Germany and were painted in 1825. Near the right wall and close to the front entrance is the original hand-hammered copper baptismal font. The font rests on a wooden pedestal, also decorated by the artist Davila, and has been placed in front of doors which will one day lead to a baptistry, yet to be restored.

Overhead are huge redwood ceiling beams which have been smoothed by hand with an adze just as was done in mission days. The tall, vaulted ceiling makes the church appear larger than it really is. Copies of the two original crystal chandeliers hang from the ceiling.

Two side altars are on the left wall of the church. The side altar nearest the sanctuary is built around one of the few objects that was saved from the 1868 earthquake. It is poly-chromed, which means painted wood, and is a statue of Saint Bonaventura. It was probably carved around 1808. In front of the sanctuary is a hand-carved wood railing copied from a piece of the original railing. At the back of the sanctuary is a lovely handmade reredos built to look somewhat like the original. A niche in the reredos holds the 15th century statue of Saint Joseph, patron saint of the mission. Today people of the area call the mission church "Saint Joseph's."

The old original cloister was once connected to the church. Some day it may once again be a part of the church building, if enough money is raised to connect the two buildings. Now the cloister sits a short distance to the right of the new church. It contains a fine, newly-remodeled gift shop and a museum, which is also a county museum. In the museum are many historical items of the Ohlone Indian tribe and from the mission itself. Since this cloister is the only remaining building from mission days, it is a treasure just as it stands. A cupboard built into the thick wall of one of the rooms nearly two hundred years ago has been left open so viewers can see how shelves were built in those days. Pieces of original plaster from the old baptistry wall are on display, as

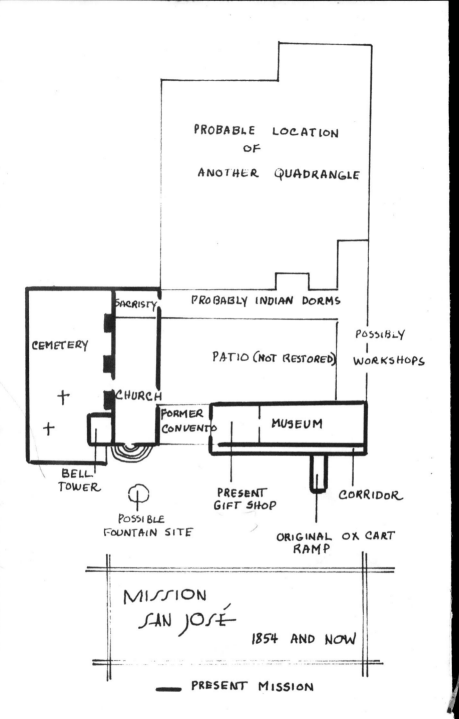

PROBABLE LOCATION
OF
ANOTHER QUADRANGLE

PROBABLY INDIAN DORMS

SACRISTY

CEMETERY

PATIO (NOT RESTORED)

POSSIBLY
WORKSHOPS

CHURCH

FORMER
CONVENTO

MUSEUM

BELL
TOWER

POSSIBLE
FOUNTAIN SITE

PRESENT
GIFT SHOP

CORRIDOR

ORIGINAL OX CART
RAMP

MISSION
SAN JOSÉ

1854 AND NOW

PRESENT MISSION

are artifacts from early days. A slide show is shown hourly telling the mission's story.

The few precious religious items surviving the earthquake were at one time displayed at the museum, but have now taken their rightful places in the new mission church. San José Mission Church which, according to its historian, Father Francis McCarthy, was not "one of the most beautiful" mission churches, but "a good, sturdy work-horse" church, is again a working parish church. This author does not agree with Father McCarthy, for the church has great beauty. The impossible has come true with the restored mission church sitting, as it should, on the old original foundation.

II. HISTORY OF THE MISSION

Mission San José was founded by Father Fermin Lasuén on June 11, 1797. The good padre knew the small town of San José was already a growing pueblo, but he hoped that the site picked for the new mission could be far enough away so city people would not bother the missionaries and their Indians. Missionary priests had learned to their sorrow that if a mission was too close to any settlement of people, the Indians became attracted to the wrong things. The new mission, after a confusing time of many names, was finally named for Saint Joseph, Patron of the Universal Church. Most newer books list the name as Mission San José de Guadalupe, but there is no record of that name in the early histories of the mission. It seems to have been named simply Mission San José.

Within two days of the founding services simple shelters had been built for the priests and soldiers. Gifts of animals and supplies from other missions arrived soon after and in three weeks there were seven more temporary buildings. They were laid out in a rectangle instead of the usual square.

Much has been written about the troublesome Indians living near this new mission. Many historians have felt that the priests had trouble with wild tribes from the very beginning. The local Indians were not really hostile. But, it must be admitted they were not eager to become part of mission life. Records show only thirty-three of them came to live at the mission the first year. The padres patiently worked with the tribes, however, and the day came when San José had more mission Indians than any other northern California mission. One of the reasons that brought Indians to the mission was the clothing given to each upon becoming a member of the mission church. Once a year every Indian received a new set of clothing and a blanket. That was quite a gift in those days.

Measles and smallpox were brought to the mission by Spanish soldiers in 1805. These diseases quickly passed to the Indians, who had no immunity because they had never been around such sicknesses before. What made the white man only ill, made the Indian die. In 18 months so many of them died, the mission population dropped from about 800 to 650. This frightened the Indians so much that many left the mission with its food and warm clothing, too afraid to live there. By 1810 there were only 545 Indians still living at San José Mission.

In 1806 Father Buenaventura Fortuni and Father Narcisa Duran arrived at the mission. For twenty years these men worked together, slowly bringing the Indians back into mission life. The padres trained their reluctant natives to be weavers, leather tanners, blacksmiths, rope-makers, tile and adobe brick makers, carpenters, and shoemakers. The Indian women learned sewing, spinning, needlework, laundering, and cooking. Some of the women helped the men by carrying adobe bricks or tiles. The priests were very kind to the women, however, and did not allow them to do heavy work.

Fr. Duran was an outstanding musician and he worked with the Indians, who truly loved music, until he had a church choir and an orchestra that performed well enough to play at other missions. Fr. Duran invented a method of writing down music so Indians could sing harmony, and some of them could actually read music. At first they made their own instruments, but eventually violins, bass viols, and flutes were sent to the mission from Mexico.

When Frs. Fortuni and Duran arrived at the mission, walls of a large new church were just being built. Work had begun the year before on this permanent church. It was designed by a priest at Mission San Juan Bautista, who was certainly not the most artistic designer of buildings. But the church had a good, solid look to it.

When the mission site was first chosen, it was known that every natural resource, from excellent soil for farming and good source of water to fine clay for making adobe, was right near at hand...except for one most important thing, trees. For some strange reason there were no trees nearby. Therefore, the job of bringing logs to the mission for ceiling beams was the biggest problem in the construction of the new church. Twenty-five miles to the north, a forest of giant redwoods was located. Five hundred of these trees were brought south to the mission with great difficulty. They were then cut into 24 foot lengths for the building of the church.

It was a very plain church, built without even the planned bell tower because of fear of earthquakes. And it was quite large: 125 feet long, 30 feet wide on the outside, with a 24 foot high ceiling inside. The walls were about eight feet thick.

The finished church was dedicated in April, 1809. By 1810, sixty permanent homes for Indians had been completed. New homes continued to be built each year until 1825, when 1,976 Indians were living at Mission San José. A monjerio, or women's dormitory, was also built in 1810. In 1811, a barracks was added for visiting military men who protected travelers from hostile Indians in the mountains close by.

In spite of diseases and occasional Indian troubles Mission San José grew. In 1816, Fr. Duran showed how shrewd a businessman he was. He obtained a boat that he used to sail some thirty miles across the bay to foreign ships anchored there. Now the mission could exchange its Indian-made products for coffee, sugar, spices, hardware, fabrics, and other much needed supplies. This very business-like arrangement made life much better at the San José Mission than at many of the other missions.

A dam was built across Mission Creek in 1819, and a flour mill was constructed there. In 1827, a soap factory and tannery were built. By that year the quadrangle was now complete. Each side was 900 feet long! The large inner patio was surrounded on three sides by buildings. A ten foot high wall was on the fourth side. The church stood in the center of the front side instead of being located in one corner, as was usual. Next to the church sat a two-story priests' quarters. Behind the quadrangle were the adobe Indian homes, a kitchen garden, an orchard, and a vineyard enclosed by ten foot high adobe walls. Behind this wall was a large water reservoir. In front of the church was an amazing fountain of hot water, coming from a nearby hot springs. The fountain was used for bathing.

In 1826 Father Fortuni, after twenty years at San José Mission, was sent to another mission. Fr. Duran, who had been chosen Father-presidente of the whole mission chain, was left with the hard job of caring for his own mission and attending to presidental business as well. There simply were not enough priests to care for the missions at this time. Mexico had broken free from Spain five years earlier and had taken over the management of the missions in California. Mexico did not send money to care for the soldiers and the missions as Spain had. The missions began taking care of their own needs, and the presidio people's needs as well.

In 1828, Fr. Duran's favorite Indian, Estanislao, who had grown up at the mission, suddenly organized some of his tribe members and turned against the mission priest. There was a terrible fight. Estanislao's group killed many soldiers but lost, finally. The soldiers wanted Estanislao killed, but Fr. Duran spoke up for the Indian and actually brought him back to Mission San José. There he lived until he died, ten years later.

Kit Carson, the famous American Indian scout, stayed at the mission for a time in 1830. In 1833, Mission San José, the richest mission in the chain at this time, was given over to a Mexican priest, Fr. Rubio. Mexico had informed all the Spanish priests they were no longer welcome at the missions. Sadly, Fr. Duran moved to Mission Santa Bárbara. Secularization laws were put into effect and the mission lands were to be given back to the Indians, leaving the priests with only the churches to care for. At least the law read this way. What really happened was that Mexican government officials bought or sold all the land they could get their hands on, keeping the money for themselves. The Indians were left to either go back to their tribal lands in the hills or to become servants to the Mexicans.

Mission San José was sold by the Mexican governor of California, Pio Pico, in 1845, for $12,000. The United States government declared the sale illegal shortly after, when California became a part of the United States. Nevertheless, it was not until 1858 that the mission buildings were returned to the Catholic Church. In the meantime, during the 1848 Gold Rush, the mission cloister became a general store and hotel. In 1853, the church became the parish church of the area and was called St. Joseph's.

A dreadful earthquake almost destroyed the large adobe church in 1868. A New England-style wooden church was built on the old church foundations. This wooden church was moved to San Mateo, across the bay, in 1982, and since that time a restoration-recreation of the original church has been going on. The history of Mission San José has come full circle with the reconstruction of the old adobe church. Wouldn't Father Duran be thrilled?

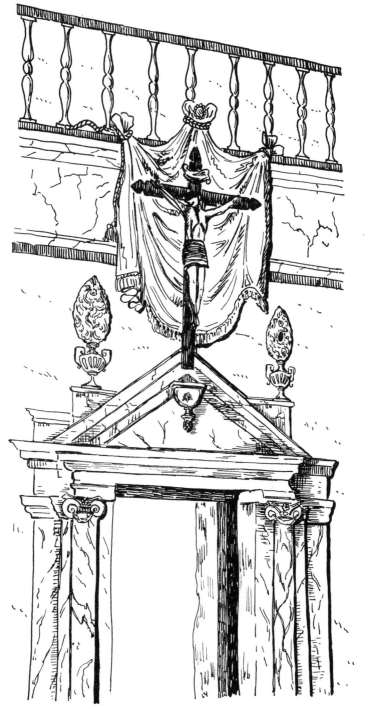

What looks to be balconies, pillars, and railings have been painted on the adobe walls in a style popular in the mid-1800s. Walls were painted by R. Menn, who copied original walls painted by Mexican artist A. Davila.

Sanctuary of newly restored mission church. Note vaulted ceiling and 15th century statue of St. Joseph, patron saint of San José Mission. The statue came from Spain.

OUTLINE OF MISSION SAN JOSÉ

I. The mission today

A. Reason for site location
B. Surroundings
C. New mission exterior
  1. Wooden church moved
  2. Adobe bricks
     a. Method of making it
     b. Number of bricks needed
     c. Plastering and painting
  3. Roof
     a. Building of under-roof
     b. Tile
     c. Nails
  4. Size of church
  5. Windows
  6. Buttresses
  7. Facade
  8. Stairs
     a. Original stairs uncovered
     b. Shape of stairway
D. Bell Tower
  1. Height and shape of tower
  2. Bells
     a. Number of bells
     b. Description of bells
E. Church interior
  1. Artist Davila's style
     a. Year of decorating
     b. Description of fresco
     c. Menn's copy of style
  2. Stations of the Cross
  3. Baptismal font
  4. Side altars
  5. Sanctuary
     a. Railing
     b. Reredos and patron saint

Outline continued next page

6. Cloister building
   a. Only original one
   b. Gift shop
7. Museum
   a. County museum of Ohlone Indians
   b. Cupboard from mission days
   c. Religious objects
   d. Slide show

II. History of the mission

A. Founding
   1. Founding
   2. Date
   3. Name of mission
B. Indians
   1. Troublesome
   2. Not eager to join mission
   3. Annual gift of clothing
   4. Diseases caught from white people
      a. Population of mission drops
C. Fathers Fortuni and Duran
   1. Number of years together
   2. Training of Indians
      a. Music of Fr. Duran
D. New church begun in 1806, finished 1809
   1. No trees nearby
   2. Beams brought from northern redwood forest
   3. Design of church
   4. Size of church
E. 1810
   1. Mission buildings description
   2. Number of Indians
   3. A boat!
      a. Trade with foreign ships
F. 1819 - 1827
   1. Dam built
   2. Soap factory and tannery
   3. Description of quadrangle
G. Fr. Fortuni leaves

H. Mexicans rule mission
  1. No money sent
    a. Soldiers depend on mission
I. Estanislao's revolt
  1. Indian attacks
  2. Father Duran's forgiveness
J. Kit Carson visit
K. Father Duran leaves
  1. Indian attacks
  2. Father Duran's forgiveness
L. Secularization
  1. Greedy officials
  2. Mission sold by Pico
M. California becomes U.S. territory
  1. Gold rush
    a. Mission is hotel and general store
  2. Church becomes St. Joseph's parish church
N. 1868 earthquake destroys church
  1. Wooden church built on foundations
O. Re-creation of adobe mission church

GLOSSARY

BUTTRESS: a large mass of stone or wood used to strengthen buildings

CAMPANARIO: a wall which holds bells

CLOISTER: an enclosed area; a word often used instead of convento

CONVENTO: mission building where priests lived

CORRIDOR: covered, outside hallway found at most missions

EL CAMINO REAL: highway between missions; also known as The King's Highway

FACADE: front wall of a building

FONT: large, often decorated bowl containing Holy Water for baptizing people

FOUNDATION: base of a building, part of which is below the ground

FRESCO: designs painted directly on walls or ceilings

LEGEND: a story coming from the past

PORTICO: porch or covered outside hallway

PRESERVE: to keep in good condition without change

PRESIDIO: a settlement of military men

QUADRANGLE: four-sided shape; the shape of most missions

RANCHOS:	large ranches often many miles from mission proper where crops were grown and animal herds grazed
REBUILD:	to build again; to repair a great deal of something
REPLICA:	a close copy of the original
REREDOS:	the wall behind the main altar inside the church
*RESTORATION:	to bring something back to its original condition (see * below)
SANCTUARY:	area inside, at the front of the church where the main altar is found
SECULARIZATION:	something not religious; a law in mission days taking the mission buildings away from the church and placing them under government rule
*ORIGINAL:	the first one; the first one built

BIBLIOGRAPHY

Bauer, Helen. *California Mission Days.* Sacramento, CA: California State Department of Education, 1957.

Baxter, Don J. *Missions of California.* San Francisco, CA: Pacific Gas and Electric Company, 1970.

Goodman, Marian. *Missions of California.* Redwood City, CA: Redwood City Tribune, 1962.

Johnson, Paul. *The Golden Era of the Missions.* San Francisco, CA 94102: Chronicle Books, 1974.

McCarthy, Fr. Francis J. *The History of the Mission San José California 1797-1835.* Fresno, CA: Academy Library Guild, 1958

Sunset Editors. *The California Mission.* Menlo Park, CA: Land Publishing Company, 1979.

Wright, Ralph B., ed. *California Mission.* Arroyo Grande, CA 93420: Hubert A. Lowman, 1977.

For more information about this mission, write to:

Old Mission San José
P.O. Box 3159
Mission San José , CA 94539-0315

It is best to enclose a self-addressed, stamped envelope and a small amount of money to pay for brochures and pictures the mission might send you.

Acknowledgements
Dolores Ferenz, Manager and Kerey Quaid, Museum Curator

CREDITS

Cover art and Father Serra Illustration: Ellen Grim
Illustrations: Alfredo de Batuc
Ground Layout: Mary Boulé

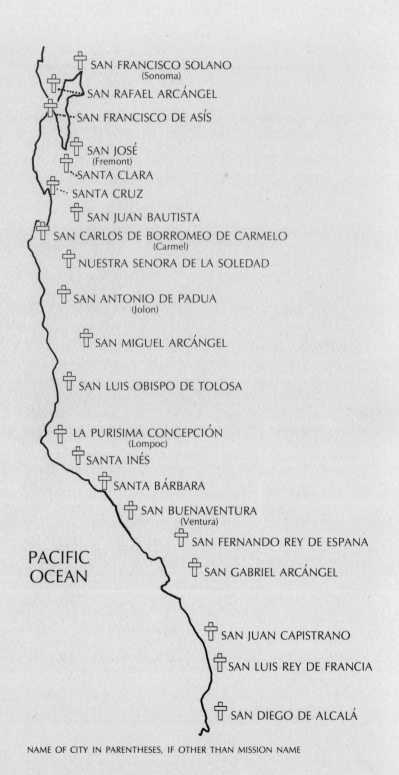

SAN FRANCISCO SOLANO
(Sonoma)

SAN RAFAEL ARCÁNGEL

SAN FRANCISCO DE ASÍS

SAN JOSÉ
(Fremont)

SANTA CLARA

SANTA CRUZ

SAN JUAN BAUTISTA

SAN CARLOS DE BORROMEO DE CARMELO
(Carmel)

NUESTRA SENORA DE LA SOLEDAD

SAN ANTONIO DE PADUA
(Jolon)

SAN MIGUEL ARCÁNGEL

SAN LUIS OBISPO DE TOLOSA

LA PURISIMA CONCEPCIÓN
(Lompoc)

SANTA INÉS

SANTA BÁRBARA

SAN BUENAVENTURA
(Ventura)

SAN FERNANDO REY DE ESPANA

SAN GABRIEL ARCÁNGEL

PACIFIC
OCEAN

SAN JUAN CAPISTRANO

SAN LUIS REY DE FRANCIA

SAN DIEGO DE ALCALÁ

NAME OF CITY IN PARENTHESES, IF OTHER THAN MISSION NAME

At last, a detailed book on the
Mission San José
written just for students

ABOUT THE AUTHOR

Mary Null Boulé has taught in the California Public School System for 25 years. Her past ten years as a fourth grade teacher made her aware of the necessity for a detailed informational book about the California missions. Five years of research, including visits to each mission, have resulted in this excellent series.

She is married and the mother of five grown children.

ISBN: 1-877599-13-1